The Moon and I

Stephen Brooke

Eggshell Boats
2021

The Moon and I

the dreams of moonlight ever fade

ISBN 978-1-937745-77-6

Eggshell Boats
is an imprint of the Arachis Press

Arachis Press
4803 Peanut Road
Graceville, FL 32440
http://arachispress.com

The Moon and I

Ring

In another life, I have
told my stories in the market,
beggar's bowl at my feet.

Hear the children toss their shiny
copper tokens in, buying
me a supper and a jug

of forgetfulness. Listen
to this tale, all you gathered
here. It was told me by one

who once sat beneath the awnings
by a blue forgotten sea, long,
long ago. Don't ask its truth.

I will only lie to you,
listening to the coins that ring,
ring, and the children's laughter.

Wares

We'll sail to where the stars
slide into the sea
and dive for them like pearls
to sell in Araby.
Yes, in spice-aired markets
of rose-colored dawn,
we'll trade our wares of wonder
before we voyage on.

And all the songs of sailors
and all the songs of night
tell of those golden cities
hid just beyond our sight.
Every song of yearning,
every song of dream,
says look to the horizons
where the South Seas steam.

We'll sail to where the moon
rises from the sea,
to fill our sails with moonlight
and cross the ebony
oceans of the nighttime
to our promised day,
to trade our wares of wonder
found along the way.

Number

I have calculated the number of elephants
needed to reach from here to the moon.
Who could round that many up?

They hide themselves in hedges and fence rows,
trumpeting their laughter. Might I
gather giraffes to fill the gaps?

Don't even ask me about Mars.

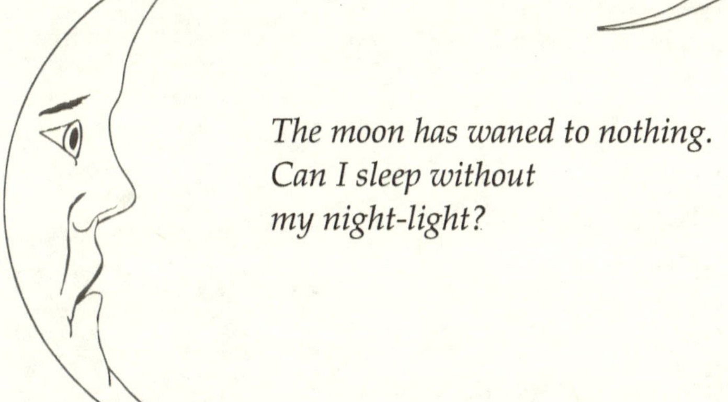

The moon has waned to nothing.
Can I sleep without
my night-light?

The Moon and I

The moon and I conversed last night
of things that were and things that might
be so some day. And we spoke on
till interrupted by the dawn;

the dreams of moonlight ever fade
before the sober sun. We made
such rhymes, the moon and I, as daft
a song as man and moon might craft,

of words that fly from star to star,
of words like fire-flies in a jar,
to be released in flashing flight
to wait beyond the doors of night,

when morning comes. The moon and I
have spoken as she crossed the sky.

as a lover
the sea yearns for the moon
rising toward her

each wave speaks its name
to the shore and recedes ~
the sea remembers

Payment

Is each word to be a coin
of payment, never flipped to know
its chance of heads or tails? When myth
is seen as dogma or as lies,

we mistranslate the very language
of our souls. For truth is painted
of many colors; God's one light
refracts, breaks apart, through angles

of prismatic perception, yet sums
to being. His music plays across
the infinite modes of chord and discord,
finding harmony with each voice.

Hear it and dance. Flip your coin
and come up on the other side
of a chance, the other side
of every payment you have made.

am I anyone
without the labels I choose
to give myself?

The Angry Music

The angry music must be heard.

Shout it, man, shout it
like it's tomorrow's truth.

Play it so it reaches
to the roofs of the moon.

All the girls will dance.

Reading

You, who thought life had no meaning:
when did you learn that it was simply
spoken in a foreign language?

The lessons have their cost. Each teacher
must be paid, a penny a word,
a dime for each vine-ripened phrase

they pick for you. And then you may
open your book, reading from
the empty pages, reading psalms

that bring the students to your feet.

Definitions

Existence is in definitions.
Tell me who I am, what I am,
or I am nothing. Name me.
Know me. The sun has a name

as does the moon. It is the start
of understanding them. Ten thousand
names later we shall know more.
Name me ten thousand times and I

begin to know who I am. Define
wings and I shall fly, lest I
fall toward the void, nameless.
Nameless and without meaning,

I am the priest, elevating
my own body at mass.
Define my presence, my substance,
in your soaring sacrifice.

Mystery is in definitions.
I carry ten thousand names
in my heart, and each
is me. Understand and be.

Anchorite

To be an anchorite
dwelling in your wastes
was all I asked; my prayers
are the diamond stars
that fill a desert sky.

Turn from me; the mountains
rise between us. Cold
comes the wind, the North Wind
breathing pestilence,
darkness, as it passes.

I renounce my world's
light, all pleasure, passion;
in solitude I chew
the withered bitter rinds
of forbidden fruit,

the lingering taste of all
my tomorrow promised.
Those mountains tower vastly,
too immensely high
to ever cross again.

Here I dwell; my desert
realm lies all about me,
a not-so-holy hermit.
Ask the stars why I
remain. They sing my prayers.

Argument

I had a disagreement with myself
  or maybe it was with my god.

We argued all night and sometimes one
  got the better and sometimes the other.

Light and bird-song spoke of the new day;
  on this, at least, we agreed.

I Seek

I seek once again the solitude of the hills.
All the day I journey nowhere and dusk
brings only the company of the uncounted stars.
The way home through night is long.
Do not ask what I have seen this day—
it was only the pines whispering to the sky.

a crescent cup ~
the moon holds water tonight
and your memory

Choir

A choir warms up, as day
cools to darkness, point
and counterpoint, soprano
screech owls answering,
echoing, the barred
baritones of the swamp.
All windows open, I dream
into the distances
of night as coyote voices
rise to join the concert.

Invention

Our names are secret. Do not whisper some
invention; I'll know it for another lie.
I'll know it as the darkened wishes, dead
within you, those you would were true.

Come, day. Come with roses and the rot
of centuries. You bear the secret name,
the name I hazard with each sun that rises
across the death of nightly comfort.

The mockingbird has sung it. The almost-words
linger. Read what is upon the grass;
wind passes, writes, erases. Read what is
when cloud forms transitory rune.

Unknown, we greet each other. I shall name
you so today and not so on the morrow.
And, tomorrow, whose voice might I hear?
My own, no other. Our names are secret.

The rain whispered
secrets to the roof all night
was my name mentioned?

Midnight Rain

The rain at midnight
drip, drip, drips,
asking me if I should rise
and close the windows.
It is not falling hard;
go back to sleep.

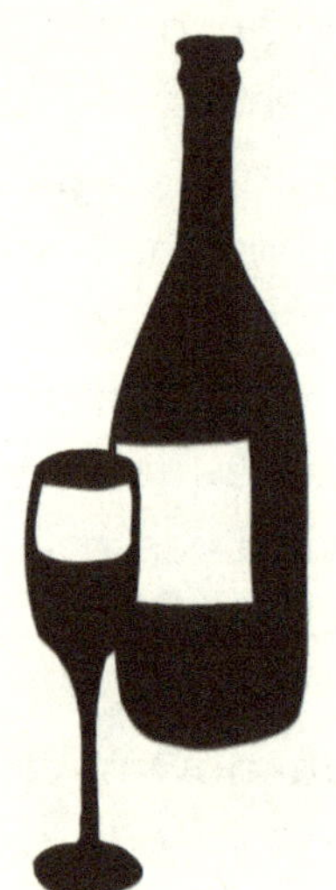

It's said the moon's made of cheese.
Is that why it goes
well with wine?

Cliche

Rain is my favorite cliche.
And night—night is good.

It rained last night.
I believe a slow train

passed by, too.

Firewood

The tree of knowledge came down
in last night's storm. Now I
must get out the chain saw,
cutting good and evil

into manageable lengths
of firewood. Will you
sit before that blaze
with me? It might burn

as brightly as the angel
guarding the gates of Eden.

Fade

I've shut the doors of night behind me;
I'll heed no more tomorrow's song.
I've heard another tune and long
To dance where dawn will never find me.

I seek that distant steady chime,
For life's elusive melody
Holds but regretful memory;
My evening star, fade this last time.

Drapes and Paint

It's the same room—I can tell.
The look has changed, the furniture moved
but I've paced off the familiar length,
measured the width, and know my cell.
Yes, yes, I know it too well,
windows, doors, that open only
onto empty mirrors and I
have no existence beyond this spell.

Or this room. I built it, you know,
for others to decorate. They say,
"Here's something new," "Here's someone new."
But it's the same: they come, they go.
It's always the same. No room to grow,
no room except this room; now you
come carrying bags and say that all
is changed, that you have made it so.

Drapes and paint won't do; you should
have brought a hammer if you understood.

I am the hole
dug in search of myself ~
fill me as you will

Question

to be or not to be—
that is not the question
but the only answer
we are given.

Couches

No couches await you, not along
the wall nor artfully angled
beneath the windows. They do not
beckon you to sit with me,

shoulder pressed to shoulder, this
or any other evening.
I have but these chairs,
cushion-filled, soft in color

and upholstery, but with
room for only one. So I
live and take my choice,
sit where I please. You may, too,

should you visit, near yet not
close, alone together,
in my rooms filled with chairs,
my many rooms that have no couches.

Windows

This house we built together
  has now grown very dark.

I can dwell in these rooms no longer
  without your familiar light.

The windows are but painted scenes
  I hung here long ago.

I have harvested today.
Why didn't I plant
tomorrow?

Soil

The mindless soil knows not
boredom and I may seek
satisfaction in dirt.

Shovel and rake, planting
and weeding and, yes, someday
I too will find its embrace

and rest.

Depart

One by one, my friends
  depart and I remain.
A wind from the mountains
  blows cold down the valleys.
One day it will carry
  all our names away.

Will

The Song of Brother Sun by Francis of Assisi
I would take over all the books of Friedrich Nietzche.

There is contentment in the beauty of one flower
that can not be attained through man's own will to power.

For powerless we come into this world, friend,
and powerless we'll be when all comes to an end.

I'll praise creation now and walk with Brother Sun,
believing in God's will until our journey's done.

Little Birds

the little birds
have not seen tomorrow
as I do

it is up to me
to worry about them

Kneads

No machine for me—
I must feel the bread
in my hands, close
my eyes and caress it,
make love with just
the right force
and the right tenderness.
And yes, I need to knead
with the yeast of four hours
rising, the sweet essence,
rising about me, a promise
of the feast to come
as the kitchen cools,
later. I do not count
the minutes, do not
watch the clock, only
feel when the time is right
to let go, to let rest.

Bread

Making bread, I could
think deep thoughts, compose
poems, symphonies,
plot best selling novels.

Instead, I lose myself
in the wordless prayers
of kneading; the silent songs
of my soul shall rise

with the loaves. In time,
I will be satisfied—
this work of making bread
may be a humble art

yet it fills a hunger.

Hammers

Without concrete blocks
and two-by-fours, who can
begin to build a house?

Once they are stacked,
what was only lines on paper,
a vacant lot, a promise,

becomes a song of hammers.

Mockingbird

The mockingbird greets the chill
  gray dawn of December.

Feathers fluffed, he seems twice
  the bird he was last summer.

How have I so dwindled
  from the man I then was?

Desire

Once, I desired life,
as a lover desires.
Once we were beautiful
together; we wore the morning

as our due, the colored,
clouds of sunrise, tumbled
as our own unmade bed.
We all run out of time

and soon I shall sleep,
as sunset fades to darkness.
Sleep, holding life in my arms
as desire also fades.

Door

I have lived in the pain of you,
knowing hurt does not outlast us,
knowing all things do come to rest,
that dusk takes each day through its door.

Shall I wait by that door, the door
that leads to night? No one sees
the whole truth of things, only
that part of it he holds close.

Let each restless dreamer wait
within, holding his torch of despair.
Who has thrown these slender daggers
at the sun? Blindly, blindly,

have I stared at his face. Let
the melancholy optimist
loosen his grip on the moon and stars.
They have only carried him home.

Tissue

Somehow, I wrapped you up
in tissue paper dreams,
only to put you away
and forget.

Entering

Who am I but you?
Spark from the same spark,
we burn with one light.

In our hearts is the dawn
and the setting sun,
the wheeling stars and moon.

Be a bird and a cage;
sing until I come
to your forgotten doors.

Entering, I free you;
and in the ache of your leaving,
you bind my heart like a wound.

Who are you but I?
Standing at the roots
of time, I speak your name.

the flower's beauty
was never meant for you ~
it beckons the bee

She Wears

This night
she wears the moon for me
and I shall rest my head
upon her silvered orbs.
The stars,
all set in ebon silk,
adorn our ceiling vault.
They find slow passage home
to dawn,
where she shall wear the sun
for me.

My Loss

Death, I do not fear;
it will come to us all,
sooner or later.

To greet that day as me
is all I ask, to not
lose the man I am

before I am not.
I have watched that loss,
seen others melt away,

and it was my loss, too.

Mortgage

Yesterday grows longer and tomorrow
far too short. I've no more time to borrow
and soon all my debts will be past due;
Life's a mortgage none of us renew.

We move from these houses, leave behind
all our suit-cases, packed with a blind
eye to death's reality. There's no
luggage carried with us where we go.

What I have, I give to you my friends;
Share it, pass it on, before life ends.

A Line or Two

You should write this poem. It's all
about you, anyway. You read,

trying to find you in the scattered
pieces of me. You read, not really

caring who I am. Come on,
take over for a line or two.

No one will know the difference

Oh, Poet

Oh, poet, feed us of your wisdom.

The words grow like mushrooms
in your cellar; they grow thick
on our refuse, the compost
of forgotten books.

Oh, poet, their flavor fills us

but we are not satisfied.
We are not nourished. They have lost
all the passion of sunlight.
The stars and the moon have

never shone on them.

Ego

I have an ego.

Even though I tell it *down, boy,*
it's apt to jump up on my guests

demanding attention.

The Universe Laughs

The universe laughs not at you and me,
my friend. We go unnoticed, specks of dust
who dream the dreams of motes, and sate our lust,
oblivious to all infinity
may find amusing. What was and will be
are met today, as it would seem they must
or not. Which does not matter; it is just
the same. It's the eternal joke, you see.

Between the stars, the laughter echoes faint
and we may strain to hear, yet comprehension
comes never. Every sinner is a saint
and every mortal, dying, seeks ascension
to heaven's promise, slipping this constraint.
The universe laughs not at our pretension.

The Stage

Tragedy and comedy
share my stage. Let the clown
fight the villain. Let him kiss
all the girls before he exits.
Hidden daggers will be wielded
soon enough. Act Three, I think.

Note

Do not ask too much of the stars;
they will not answer when you
call roll, and Rigel is not here
tonight. His mother sent a note.

The Other Me

I have thought more than once
of that well-worn cliche:
but for the grace of God,
there go I, on my way.

Might I have been a beggar,
had life made other turns,
and live beneath some bridge,
be one all mankind spurns?

I could give thanks to Fortune,
I should thank God above,
and certainly I must
thank those who've shown me love,

but in the Infinite,
I know all things will be,
and on some street, somewhere,
there begs that other me.

Monkey King

Life is a tree-full of monkeys
and I am the king of them all!
I climb to the highest of branches,
I know where the best fruits will fall.
Each monkey girl adores me,
they come to me when I might call;
Is anything better than being
a king in a tree standing tall?

I am the king of the monkeys,
against me no others avail,
for I have the sharpest of teeth,
the longest and most curly tail.
And if by misfortune I spy
the face of some poor lesser male,
I chase him along leafy ways;
the monkey king never shall fail!

Life is a tree-full of monkeys,
where I sit high on my throne;
the females all vie for my grooming,
so I don't sit there alone!
I'm sure I shall be king forever,
the greatest that my kind has known—
the mightiest monarch of monkeys,
and no tree as fine as my own!

Hidden

Hiding! Abiding! The goblins in their caves!
Rolling! Gamboling! The mermaids 'neath the waves!
Ah, but men are blind
and little do they find,
fleeing, unseeing, from birth unto their graves.

Peeping! Unsleeping! The fairies in the trees!
Wailing! Unfailing! The banshee on the breeze!
But men stumble on
until their days are gone,
drinking, unthinking, their cup down to its lees.

Lurking! Smirking! The troll beneath his bridge!
Howling! Prowling! The wolf-kind on the ridge!
Men will shut their eyes,
counting themselves wise—
sneering, while fearing, is man's heritage.

Sorrow! Tomorrow! It comes to mortal men!
Laughter! Long after! Hear the fading din!
Ever live the fay,
beyond our end of day.
Hidden! Forbidden! Unknown, our fairy kin!

all the best stories
happened once upon a time
in lands far away

Distant

A distant storm arises, dark and full of thunder
on some horizon. Far away; there is no need
to look beyond our selves, no reason we should heed
that whispered warning rumble. Let tomorrow blunder

into today, as ever. Lightning does strike twice
eventually and we stand waiting, waiting on
each naked hilltop. All the rain has come and gone
yet surely comes again; we need but roll our dice

and hit the luckiest number. Roll them as the thunder
rolls distantly but don't look up. There is no need.

Vacancy

Will you dwell
in the empty rooms
of my heart?

I have cleared
them of yesterday's
furniture,

worn memories
wrapped in verse and left
at the curb.

Nothing

Everything is real.
Otherwise, it would
be nothing. Is nothing
part of everything?

Maybe. I should count
my nothings and see how many
I have. Not that it matters;
they still add up to nothing.

Wrappings

My prayer, many the restless
night, is to sleep
and not wake. The sun
is only God's latest taunt;
the morning, His brightly wrapped
package of despair.

How many empty boxes
have I opened before?
Now the ribbons are pressed
between my pages, the papers
carefully folded. And why
not? They're all I have.

Towers

Each tower topples, some
silently, some in furies
of stone and tears. And I
will build anew,

laying up walls of want
and wish, for I know
heaven is not beyond
man's reach. I know

for I've dreamed. One day,
I'll knock again upon
those gates. Would you
open them to me?

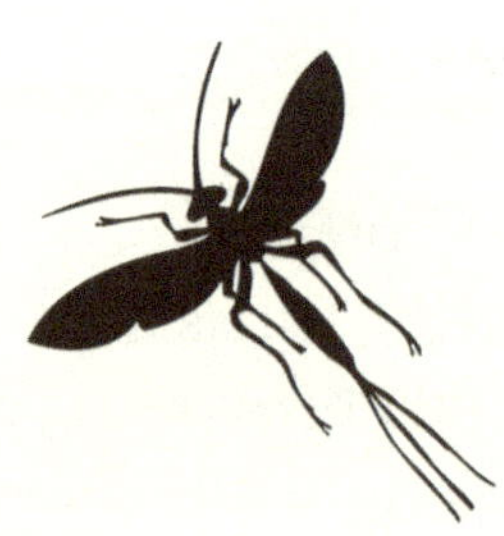

Mayfly Poem

Mayflies danced upon the water and disappeared.
Summer days also came and went in their swarms.
You, as well, are gone and days grow short,
and now only wine and fire warms

this heart, longing for the season passed.
Mayflies dance and die—I sit and drink.
Every poem I wrote for you is finished;
summer is now memories and ink.

Forests

The fruit contains the seed.
From the seed grows the tree.
The tree bears the fruit.

I have planted
with the rising sun.
I have awaited the rain.

Hope is the seed.
Faith is the tree.
Love is the fruit.

I have tasted the day.
When evening wraps herself
in blue, come to me.

Tomorrow ripens.
Its seed will be scattered
across our empty hills.

I have blessed the night,
giving thanks for each
rising star.

We shall be forests,
tall and fruitful, dreaming
against the sky.

Nests

Different degrees of madness
divide us: you from me,
him from her from them.
Each has his own losses.

Each heart's an empty bird's nest,
broken, trampled where
it fell. How will we seek
the life that might have filled it?

Only in the lies
and the truth that lies
between the lies; only
in stories of our madness

are the discarded shells
of dreams once hatched and flown.
Do they nest again,
somewhere, those birds of loss?

Only the degrees
that divide us know
their song. Listen for it;
listen in the forests.

Listen in the dawn
and remember. You've heard it
before, heard its echo
in your empty places.

Listen and know they've flown
beyond your reach. Different
degrees of madness divide us.
Each has his own losses.

Only Wind

The tongues of the forest
spoke your name
in leaves of memory,

tumbling, tumbling,
as I burnt with them
to the sky.

Only wind
could hold us, singing you
across the day

and into never.

Sermons

The mockingbird on the brush-pile
disapproves of the one
high in the peach tree.

Each mounts his pulpit perch
to denounce the other, to preach
a sunrise sermon of song.

Any morning, I willingly
attend this church.

Wordless

To wordless sing, I go into the day
you leave behind. Beyond this sham of dawn,
beyond the dew yet sparkling on the lawn,
sunrise surrenders, leaving only gray.

All murmured in the dark now fades away
so soon, so soon, still must I choose to sing—
I shall be as a bird, awakening,
and wordless go; what more have I to say?

Ripe

The last ripe peach will go
unpicked. Let it fall as fall
the days, one after the other,
fall into the heat of August.

Haze fills these mornings, too thin
to claim the name of fog.
There is no chill to it.
The sluggish sun hides, bides,

blurs the bounds I have set
on work and sleep and rest,
and I too must fall
into another August day.

I have seen the last fruit
tumble to the grass,
all its sweetness untasted.
The day will carry it away.

cicada trill breaks
the hushed heat of noon and fades
again to silence

Sinews

I will run until I
forget, slam the heavy
bag, make myself weary
with curls and presses.

I have searched for sleep
in pills and bottles,
forgetfulness in the pursuit
of illusive pleasures,

but found nothing, save within
the singing of my own sinews.

Web

What wayward, winged thing were you
that blundered into my cobwebbed
desire? What dream of destined love
led you to flutter there? The spider

who once dwelt in these rags is gone,
dried up and blown away. Now, only
the husks of other fools dance here,
in soft ballet upon the breeze.

Redbud

Amid familiar red and brown
an unexpected hue appears.

I watch pink blossoms fly away,
borne on the autumn winds.

Indian summer has tricked the redbud;
in my heart, spring still sleeps.

the candle I lit
at noon added nothing
to the sun

The Old Samurai

Every enemy
is dead, save time.

What need have I now
of this sword,

other than to fall
upon it?

Splinter

A splinter of God
might be named *today*
or *Elizabeth.*

When it dies
it forgets its name.
Who were you?

we ask. *Weren't*
you God, last week?
If a rainbow's

seven colors
refract through the facets
of memory,

shall we call
this splinter *yesterday*?
Do not speak

that name quite yet;
wait until I too
forget and may

be forgotten.
Until our fire turns
to splintered stars.

The Open Way

Burdened with your miracles
and signs, I seek the open way.
My feet trod there once, where shadow
mingled with the void, where peaks
lost themselves in endless sky.
The stars swarm yet above; I glimpse
them shining, unknown constellations,
that form and fade, and can not guide.

The hand of time rests on my shoulder;
the way home is over there,
comes a voice. We could walk
together. We could watch the sun,
watch it rise and set again,
and the coming of a star-clad
night that surely follows. Walk.
Walk into its welcoming dark.

Moonlight has set the birds to song;
they mount to treetop, greet the dawn
come too soon, in silvered guise.
They call out baffled challenges,
singing to their shadowed world.
Sleep will call them back, in time,
back to the nest they have defended
against the moon, against the night.

Who counts the waves on empty beaches?
Each speaks its name; each writes it in
the wind-lost foam and only the sea
remembers. I recede as the wave.
Who will know my name tomorrow?
Who counts the days before they blow
away, across the timeless depths?
Walk the empty beach with me.

Count on; no finite number can
contain that which is infinite.
One is One, a part, a whole,
at once and never. On in limping
pursuit, add One to One to One,
and time will end before you draw
any closer. Limit God;
make him a number and count on.

I close my eyes to every sign,
to the beckoning stars. The landmarks
are all lost, the skies adrift.
My way leads through the songs we learned
in the womb; our mothers' hearts
told the rhythm. To exist
is miracle enough, to be,
the only sign we ever needed.

Then, the open way was not
so hard to find, yet ever easy
to lose. I search remembered skies
for hidden, shifting chasms of cloud,
for sun and moon and fading songs.
The road must rise and lead away;
as surely as the day finds night
and sleep, it will lie before me.

Reach

All my dreams, stacked up,
never reach far enough.
The star atop the Christmas
tree, when I was small,

sang beyond my grasp.
My heart yearned to hold,
to keep it for myself—
so many other stars since,

so many elusive stars.
My arms and my dreams
have grown tired; I'll reach
so far no more. Ha,

until tomorrow night
when more stars fill my skies.

The Sixties, Again

There was an anger and an innocence, then,
served up buffet-style on the radio
and on the back of album sleeves and the pages
of underground magazines and newspapers.

We feasted, you and I, never caring
that it might be too much, that tomorrow
will throw regrets at such easy targets.
Let the cynics come; they always do

and one decade follows another. Maybe I
saw it before you, in the shadows we cast.
The fading reverb of Dick Dale's Strat
haunted those years, forgotten but felt,

echoed in our heart beat, in every wave
that broke and ran back to the sea,
in every trip to those far misted shores.
They beckoned us, they did, and we followed

our white rabbits while we could and our youth
disappeared down one hole or another. Across
each song I have sought it, through
cartoon pop and slick pseudo-psychedelia.

Again, the Sixties—no one saw them leave
but I knew they were gone. They became lost
in the jungle gunfire, to be identified
by their dog-tags, identified as the children

who danced the surfer-stomp when night was still
a friend. Pointless is as pointless does;
we both know it never mattered. Yes, the music
was good but it never mattered at all.

Patrick Pier

Across A-1-A from Patrick Pier
the pilots practiced landings and takeoffs,
turboprops a-shriek as they passed overhead.
We held our ears and waited on waves,

anticipating our own takeoffs.
We, too, could fly, fly down green faces,
no more earth-bound than any pilot.
The pilings disappeared years ago,

the last lone sentinels of a realm
demolished by the sea. Do the kids
today remember the name? Do they know
of mornings when Broncos took off and landed

and lines rolled in at Patrick Pier
and that was enough? I'll point it out
someday, if we drive up that way,
even if there is nothing to see.

Wrens

Young wrens buzz, buzz, buzz from tree to tree,
trying out their wings. I send only words
flying, seeking nests beyond these woods.
Will I ever trust enough to follow?

last year's wasp nest ~
a fragile paper platform
for this year's wren nest

Trumpet

A stir! A blur of wings—one hummingbird
seeks morning's scarlet trumpets, where the vines
have reached across, linked peach tree to magnolia.

Her jeweled green yet gray in dawn, she seeks
the nectar-sweetened colors of the sun,
amid the diamond dew on leaf and web.

A sip, side-slip to the next siren blossom—
she seeks the songs of life within each trumpet.
I've heard their promise echo into day.

God's migrant labor
comes to pick this year's crop
and then move on

seeking fresh employment
in a flurry of gray wings

Vulture

I've read you are of the kindred of storks—
that's what the scientists claim who counted
out your genes like beads on an abacus
and added them up to *Cathartidae*.

Once, we thought you cousin to the hawks
and falcons, their not-so-reputable
relative with bad table manners
and monotonous taste in tailoring.

Soar. I will still watch you circle
higher into the infinite blue
and from this distance you are more
of the angels than aught else.

indigo shadows
stretch into tomorrow ~
a distant owl calls

Shards

What words? None complete this,
none carry me far enough.
I only fling what I have
into the waiting darkness.

Much goes unsaid; that has
ever been so. We can but chip
away at the infinite,
display our shards and pretend

to wisdom. Surely knowing
something, saying something,
has, too, its value.
So what if the gods laugh

at our pretenses? There are
things beyond them, as well.

Woodpeckers

Black and white flashes high in the trees.
Red bobbing and bobbing amid the green.
The woodpeckers seek their home in the spring.
I walk on, having no place to nest.

Stacks

Speak riddles. I shall seek
what answers you need,
bring stacks of words
that might make sense

if that one in the middle
were moved but then
the whole thing would
fall and I'd never get

them in order again.
No matter. Let me scribble
pictures of my soul,
shingle your roof

with post-it notes.
The rain will sing you
to sleep in the arms
of my words.

among the cypress
the laughter of woodpeckers
echoes into spring

Black Hole

All falls in; the black hole at the center
of my being draws a universe
to itself in misted star-thick spirals,
inward, disappearing, disappearing.

All falls in, toward nothingness, suspended
timelessly on some event horizon
of my making, vanishing, existing,
in the mirrors of its paradox.

What exists, what save the self reflected,
neither here nor there, destroyed, intact?
All falls in, sinks to that empty center,
where once burned a light to fill the heavens.

Starve

Death is at your shoulder.
He would take you, whisper you
away in a cold
exhalation. He would

take you on my watch,
starve your days
like the blank-eyed beggars
that reach toward me.

I place coins
in their hands but they
will not be fed.
Death is at your shoulder,

holding the prayers of memory.
Spread singing on the table,
you did not eat.
They only grow cold.

Spaces

I am the empty space
to fill with yourself,
poured in like morning coffee.
Sugar and milk? I ask

and ruin it. Pour me
out again and this time
I'll keep quiet and all
the times that come and go

through all the empty spaces
I can be. Shapeless,
meaningless, nameless—
know me by my absence.

Promise

Life, I do not ask
that you keep each promise;
only that you make
some I might believe.

Tell me pleasant lies,
pour my glass half-full.
I think you will find me
easy to deceive.

I'll yearn for each sunrise,
as each that came before.
Life, make me a promise,
one I might believe.

Statues

Let the statues of great men come down.
Trees provide more inspiration, give
better shade. Children climb them more
easily. No one doubts their politics.

Let the trees rise where great men once stood,
in the parks, along sun-dappled streets,
guardians more sure than those cold heroes.
Let them reach toward god for each of us.

Threads

I unravel threads torn from my sanity,
weaving garments pleasing to your vanity;
now the monk's black cowl conceals a motley jester,
hides a heart of holiest profanity.
In pretense of prayer, I seem oblivious
to your whispered words, depraved, lascivious;
deep within my soul the leering ape ancestor
howls and mocks this pretense of humanity.

When a muted love speaks its ambivalence,
let me don the garb of gaudy eloquence;
choose some torn and tailored suit of my despair,
yet another patch upon my reticence.
These remain my secrets, these remain my lies;
these are sins I must keep hidden from your eyes.
Which of my fine empty rags shall next I wear,
best to clothe the silence, feigning innocence?

As unravel threads, my ill-stitched seams will fray;
I come ever to you in such disarray,
all my nakedness veiled in false modesty
tracing steps of my own decadent ballet.
For each lover will become the one in time
and, together, name the price paid for this crime;
then in penitent's robes, seeking amnesty,
shall I doff the tangled threads of yesterday.

Surface Tension

With each slow breath I wonder when
this boundary might collapse and I
sink into you, our surface tension
broken. Fixed between the depths

and sky, I spar with my reflection,
certain it grows slower, merges
into liquid, formless, dark
beneath me. Will some breeze-born ripple,

errant breath, disturb our balance,
and I disappear at last?
This shimmering of surfaces,
illusion of solidity,

disintegrates beneath my feet.
Step forward; step and do not sink.

the fragrant ashes
of your incense blew away
to join yesterday

Feast

It is what it is and I could
be thankful or I could curse
all the days until now and all
the days that stretch ahead
and it will be what it will be
as it was what it was. A feast
has its chewed bones and the dog
will be thankful for those.

But I indulge myself, this day, no
more than any other. It is not
my way to heap high my plate
nor to return for seconds. Let
the strangers at my table replace
themselves, year by year, each like
the one before, and who they are
is who they are. I toast them all.

See how the dark meat and the white
have been divided, platters of take-your-choice,
make-your-choice, cut carefully
from the carcass of time. There is
never enough time, they say, nor thyme
in this stuffing to become fully
seasoned. Feast on these, giving
thanks that it is what it is.

Thanksgiving

Shall I give thanks for all
the things I never wanted,
for which I never asked?

I'd just as soon return them,
have naught, be not. Yet here
they are, these empty gifts,

unopened boxes, clutter
to fill the corners of life.
No matter; leave them there.

Leave them and give thanks.

Toy

I am God's broken toy,
passed on to his younger brother.
He dresses me in motley
to be the fool in his puppet shows,
then forgets me.

Yesterday, I learned a song
from the roaches in his closet.
It goes "hmmmmmmmm."
Sing with me.
Hmmmmmmmmm.

walking shaded paths
I write poems in my head
to carry home

the one I meant for you
was lost along the way

I no longer write
love songs, except now and then
when I think of you

Swimmer

Time's ocean swallows every swimmer stroking
toward desired distant shores; once
glimpsed, their promise draws us on, to sink
into cold unknown depths. What song is that,

calling me? Whose voice goes whispering
across the darkened waves? Only mine,
echoed by the soaring, seeking gulls.
Encompassing our fragile lands of birth

and death, encircling each who strives. Time's ocean
lies unbounded, leaden. Struggle on,
swimmer; follow every setting sun
to its horizon, every sullen wave

to its breaking. The days forget their names
on those hidden coasts, forget them as
I have forgotten mine. I whispered once
into the wind and it was borne away.

I know all too well
the sadness in your heart ~
we are both human

Sift

My sky is broken.
The wandering planets
swim randomly
between too-distant stars.

Why have they abandoned
the courses I knew,
the fixed future
they always foretold?

This moon waxed and waned
all in one night.
Did I kiss you then
or was that another?

God has fallen asleep.
The heavens sift
in slow disarray
from his open hand.

An ocean flows through our veins.
What tides carry us
to our shores?

Crossed

How wide lie the seas we cross unknowing
on the voyages of dream? What misted
isles below escape our eyes, turned ever
to the fabled coasts beyond, yet hiding

in the fierceness of their tropic sunrise?
There behind the night they wait, the still air
fragrant with tomorrow's promised waking.
And below, the formless isles call to us:

'Tarry not, oh travelers, ye sailors
of the night! Our castaways sleep dreamless
here, unable to go on.' Their whispers
fade into the darkened sea, yet sighing

onto nameless, fog-hid sands. A dawning
murmurs in the east, in songs tinged Tyrian
and gamboge, above the long-sought city,
golden domes and spires yearning skyward,

jeweled streets awakening. Throw open
your bazaar, oh promised port of dreaming.
I have brought the stars to trade; I plucked them
where they shone upon the ebon water

Thank you for reading THE MOON AND I. I hope you have enjoyed this collection of my poems. ~ *Stephen Brooke*

Stephen Brooke is a poet, novelist, artist, and sometime surfer, residing in the Florida Panhandle.
http://stephenbrooke.com

Other poetry titles by Stephen Brooke,
all available from the Arachis Press:

Pieces of the Moon
Dreamwinds
Retellings
The Tower
Fields of Summer
Awful Alvin and Other Peculiar Poems (Juvenile)
Voyages
Magic
A Poet's Day

Eggshell Boats is an imprint of the Arachis Press
http://eggshellboats.com
http://arachispress.com

www.ingramcontent.com/pod-product-compliance
Lightning Source LLC
LaVergne TN
LVHW050944080826
845145LV00004B/1405

* 9 7 8 1 9 3 7 7 4 5 7 7 6 *